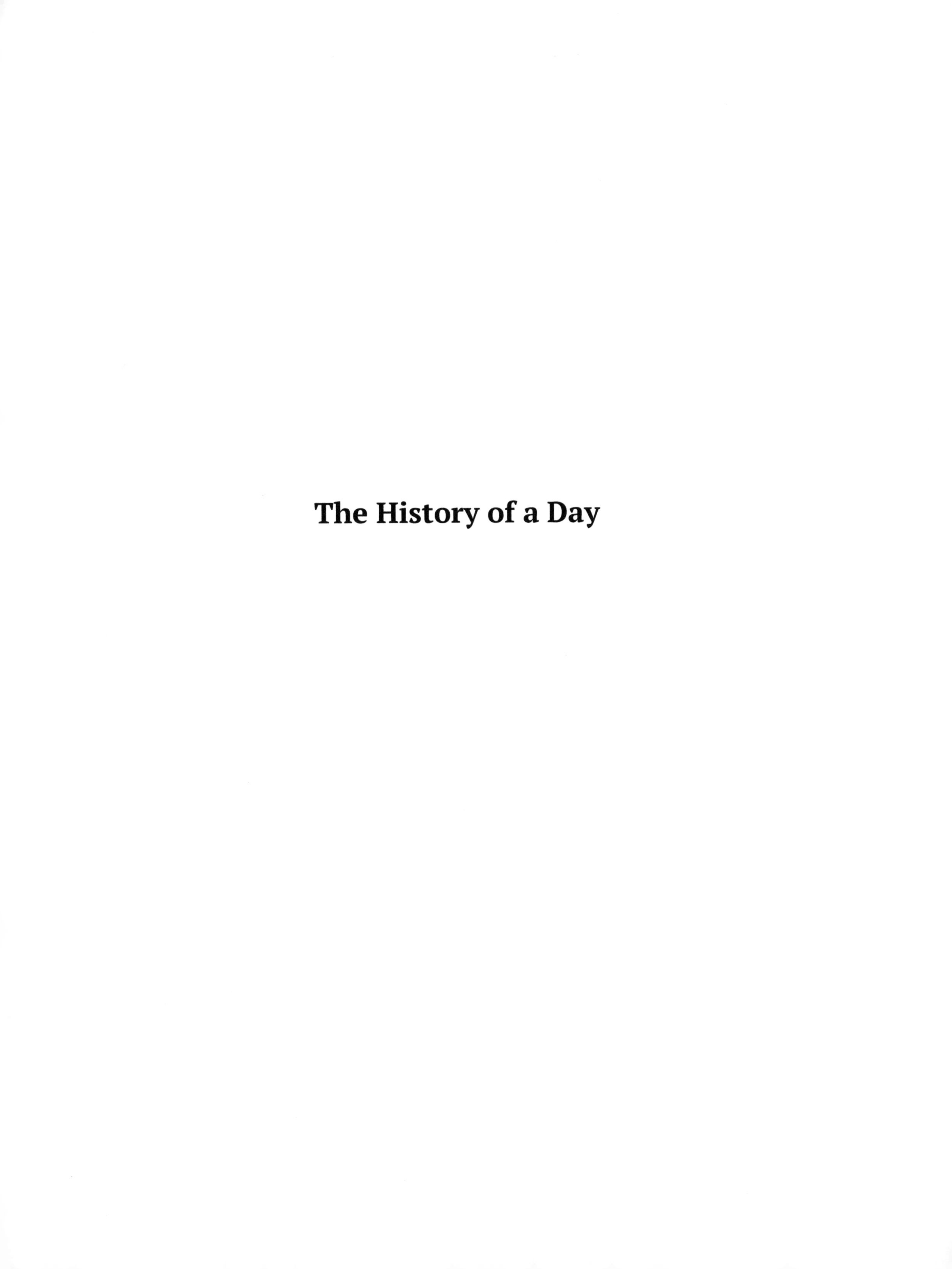

The History of a Day

All art by Bill Hoover

Cover design by Jill Rizzo

Book design by Jen Lambert & Liz Kay

ISBN 978-0-9897837-3-6

Published by burnt books, an imprint of Spark Wheel Press

The History of a Day

Bill Hoover

burnt books

Omaha, Nebraska

To the 12 writers for their extraordinary interpretations,

To Bob Hoppe for his organization and encouragement,

To Stacia for her faith and love,

Thank you

The History of a Day

The Nottingham, completed in 1925, is listed on the National Register of Historic Places. The application for historic designation described the Nottingham as the only known Tudor Revivial "L" Court Garden Apartment in Omaha, Nebraska, and was cited as an excellent example of an apartment building that used iconic details and modern conveniences. Located at 33rd & Burt streets, the three-story structure was completely renovated in 2013.

My painting is inspired by these apartments where I lived for a number of years in the late 1980s and early '90s. The Nottingham was filled with artists and addicts, poets, musicians, students and scofflaws.

I invited 12 writers I admire to choose one of the apartments I painted and interpret what they saw. The result is this collection of poems, short stories and a play. Each writer's unique take on the images brought new life to the painting. It is my hope that the images come to life for you as you enter "The History of a Day."

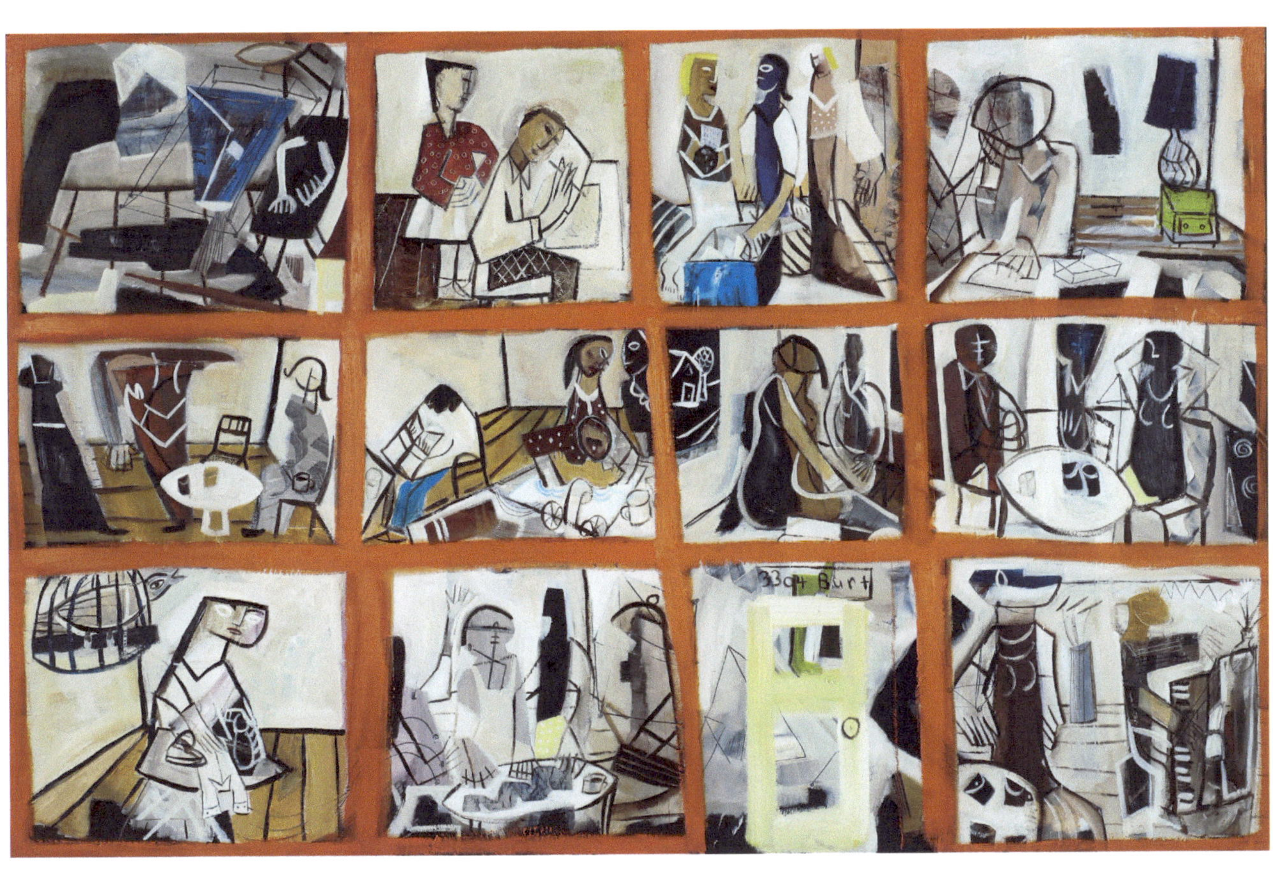
3304 Burt

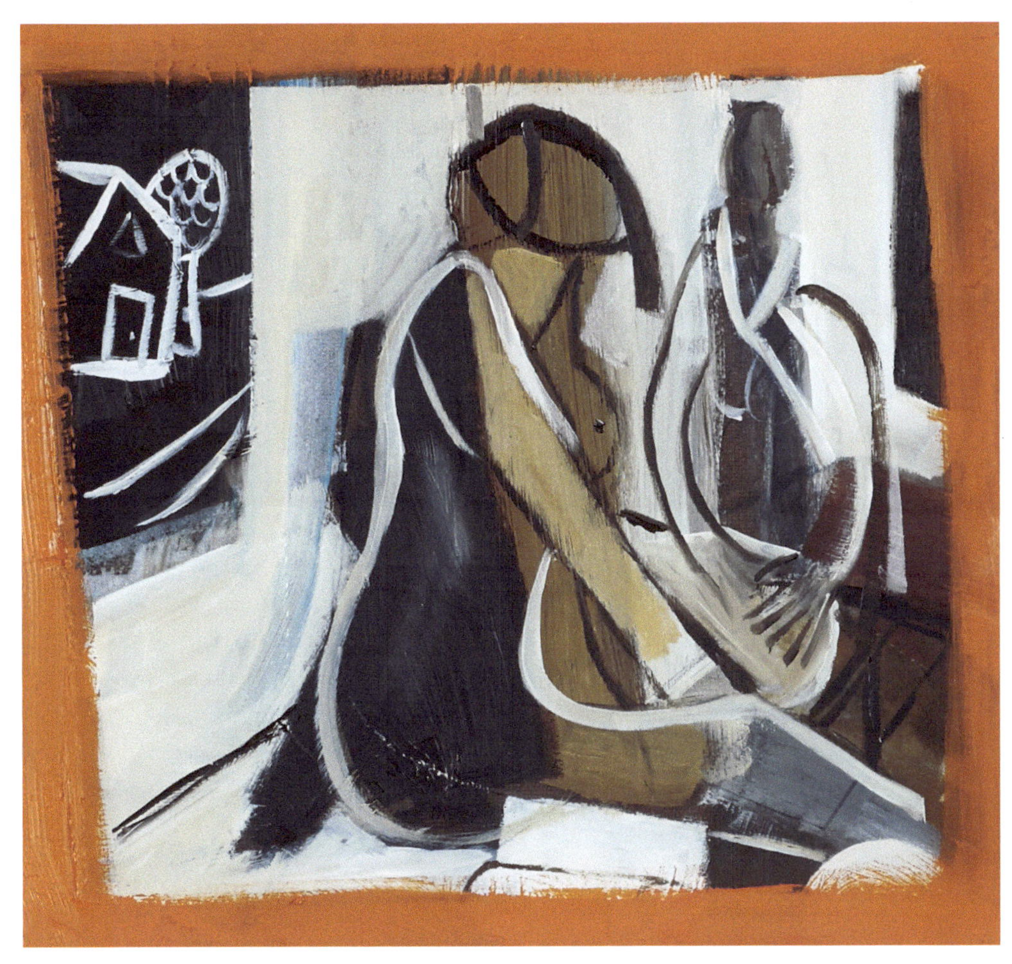

Determined to Be a Somebody | Brittany Young

Face to the window
While I'm talkin' to my kinfolk.
Thinking back to the days
The kids came to my window
And asked me to play.

They said,
"Come out, come out
Wherever you arrrrrre!"

But I was hiding in the shade
Too afraid
That they would see my true shades.

I felt like the whole world was in color
But I'm stuck in gray,
'Cause I'm not livin'
I'm just...passing days.

Maybe just maybe
I'll come out of hiding someday.
But why does that someday
Always seem to be so far away?

What's this talk about change?
Is it just a phase?
I been talkin' resolutions
Every 365 days.

Yet I'm sitting here,
Still hiding behind this window pane.
Saying no to life
When it asks me to come out and play.

But I'm done being stuck
On old news and replays.
You 'bout to see my best play.
I'm coming off the bench today...

Determined to be a somebody
Instead of a someday.

So have a seat and let me speak,
I'm getting stronger by the second.
I'm breaking off these chains,
Stopped giving in and second-guessing.

You could say I learned my lesson.
I guess I should've studied,
'Cause without wisdom and truth
My vision gets so dark and fuzzy.

I lifted up my head
'Cause I'm the head and not the tail,
So I quit playing Simon Says
And started blazing my own trail.

So from now on when you see me
Walking into 3304 Burt St.
You'll see me
Walking out my dreams.

'Cause I'm done being stuck
On old news and replays.
You 'bout to see my best play.
I'm coming off the bench today...
Determined to be a somebody
Instead of a someday.

Brittany Young is a poet, entrepreneur, and social innovator. She is founder of Brittany Young Enterprises, a communications entity consisting of inspirational media, workshops, and performing arts. She is also co-founder of The Start Center, a nonprofit organization empowering urban communities through entrepreneurship and talent development.

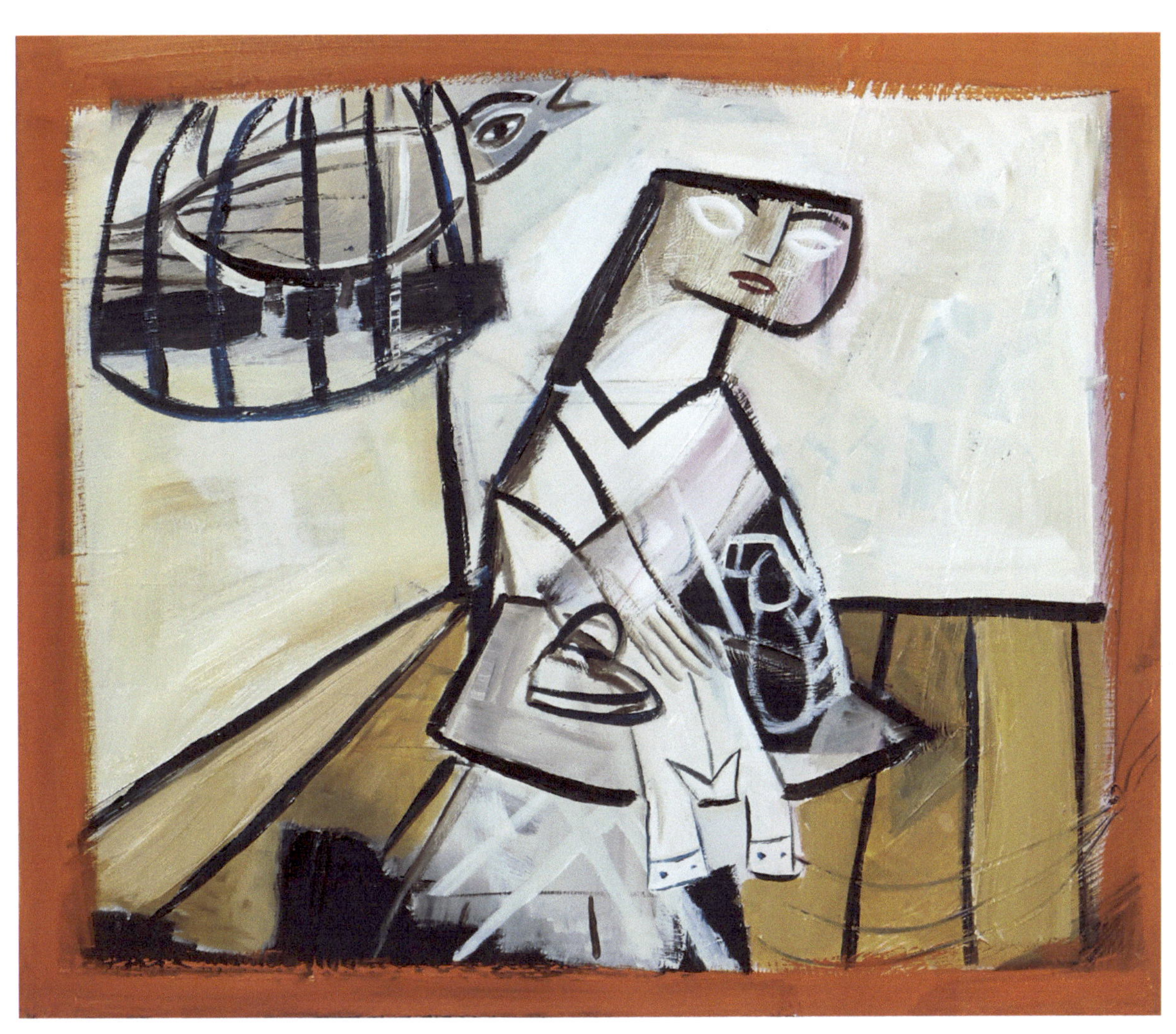

Hopeful Monsters | Miah Sommer

Scene: Interior of spare bedroom of a midtown apartment. Lucy, a thirty-something wife, irons a man's shirt in the room used for this purpose as well as to house the annoying bird that came with the marriage.

Lucy (addressing her ironing): I know the forms that love can take.

(A well-dressed man in his mid forties appears from off stage.)

Man: She focuses on the eradication of topographical lines on cotton. There is an odd pleasure she gets from performing this task for her husband, a task that any ape could perform with little to no training. Yet she feels no resentment. Acts of service, after all, ARE her love language. She ponders the state of her marriage. She sees herself as an observer, like a photojournalist, who has reached the point of neutral observer. She wonders: If there truly is a natural passion mechanism that drives men and women to pair for life, what happens to it? Does it go away completely? Does it take on a new form? She pretends to know the answers to the questions that in all actuality she does not truly understand. Most of her theories as of late have, in her opinion, been spot-on gems. Theories such as:

Lucy: You know that intense passion we all feel at first? That's basically an Assyrian god . . . you know?

Man: And . . .

Lucy: Mature love is an Australopithecine. It is a bipedal, tree-dwelling hominid.

Man: This is where she has landed today.

Lucy: That kinda sounds right, even though I'm not entirely certain what it means. Do we, as humans, have unrealistic expectations of love? If love is a byproduct of nature trying to trick us into procreation, what are the wages of that? . . . I'll tell you what they are, it's that nature owes us no apologies. We are meant to perpetuate the species and anything that happens after the passion and steady lovemaking have subsided is up to us.

(She pauses, staring at the shirt for ten seconds in thought.)

Lucy: Nature couldn't care less what we do after it has used us up?

(She starches the collar. She seems quite into the act, but stops suddenly and addresses her audience.)

Lucy: Love is liquid. Love finds its own level. Love has fucking flow. This can make love exceedingly difficult to locate. Especially if one possesses an unrealistic, overly rosy view of what love is.

Man: This is the very view she has possessed for a large chunk of her life.

(The man moves slightly more center.)

Man: As a flushed-cheeked, knobby-kneed tween she had the same fantasies and illusion of love as all the others of her awkward ilk. The beginnings of her middle school years led to books newly wrapped in brown paper bags. These were blank canvases that awaited her graffiti, the names of her loves. The hard, Teutonic alliteration of Kevin Krug's name had the same power written as it possessed when spoken aloud.

Lucy (softly and dreamily, stressing her K's): Kevin Krug.

Man: His rebellious indifference to long division was viewed as a sign of derring-do, and not for the learning disability that it truly was. She even had the distinct honor of landing the role of Becky to his Tommy in the playground reenactment of the made for TV movie "Coward of the County" based on the hit song by Kenny Rogers. At this point in her understanding, love was as ambiguous as a mammalian fetus. It could be a squirrel, a horse, or a human. It was really too soon to tell. However, of one thing she was certain: Love was both intense and forever.

Lucy (again softly and dreamily, stressing her K's): Kevin Krug.

Man: As an astute chronicler of her longings and inner workings she had seen the leaves turn on lust as a concept. This was not viewed with complete disbelief. It was, after all, a marriage and as such it was subject to the vicissitudes of nature just like any other animal behavior. Even though there was no historical precedent, history itself had provided explanations.

Lucy: It is a bit tempestuous isn't it? New love.

(She grabs a different, but completely identical shirt.)

Lucy: Like most people, I see many parallels between modern love and the gods of the ancient Near East.

Man: She believed this to be a true statement.
Lucy: Think of the gods of Egypt. They were benevolent for the most part. Sure they had an asshole god or two, but by and large they were kind, almost avuncular. Conversely, in Mesopotamia, their gods were cruel fuckers who would destroy humans for the slightest transgression. Do you know why the god destroys humankind in the Epic of Gilgamesh? Because they made too much noise! If you look at what the catalyst was for these gods you just have to look at the unpredictable nature of the Tigris and Euphrates rivers. Prone to sudden violent floods seemingly out of nowhere; it's understandable that the gods they created were tempestuous and capricious. This is essentially the stormy intensity of new love, don't you think?
But the Nile, the Nile was the giver of life. Its predictable ebbs and flows made the Egyptians feel as if their god was a happy god; not given to fits and shit-shows. Love, mature love, long-lived love is the Nile. Predictable? Sure. Boring? Perhaps. But when you live along its banks, that is the only way you want it. How do we, on a consistent basis, figure out the trick to making it from the furor of new love to the sometimes unknowable contentment of aged love? What we learn of love does not prepare us for this scenario.

Man: Like many of her contemporaries she was ostensibly filling the gaps in her knowledge of real love from pop culture. The songs of the '80s spoke of a love so great that it crumbled the foundations of loyalty to friends, even really great friends like Jesse. The intense feeling made the loving, the touching, and even the squeezing seem worth the duplicity. Eventually she began to see that perhaps pop music and romantic comedies did not contain the answers to age-old questions. Perhaps, even, there was something slightly false about it.

Lucy: It did not take into account that 30 years later, even though this is the man I love more than anyone in the world, I can tell you that if he clears his throat again, I might never stop stabbing him. Ever.

Man: This transition could be painful at times. She thought of the kisses she received from her husband 15 years ago. Those kisses meant something different. They meant that he was interested in her, in knowing her -- her favorite books, movies, what her family was like, her dreams, what she was like as a kid. The kisses still mean love, but often this variety of love is so docile that the kisses feel as if they mean "I better kiss you in case you are decapitated in a car accident on the way home."

Lucy: I remember in the beginning I had this huge nervous energy over what we would be wearing. I got so nervous, hoping he would like what I was wearing. Wearing a dress for the first time would make me giddy with anticipation. I couldn't wait to see him; it was all fresh then. Now, he knows every single article of clothing that I own. He has seen me so often that it probably feels like he is looking in a mirror . . . (She pauses, then deeply sighs.) . . . and now I basically dress him, so . . . (She shrugs and trails off.)

Lucy: But isn't it true that love, even though nature didn't intend for it to be permanent, it evolved, persevered, and expanded its life span? Consider the Australopithecus.

Man: (He extends his upturned palm to her.)

Lucy: Well look at the whole human family tree. With each step we had some pretty, cool, positive adaptations. But with each cool innovation we had to give some things up. We now walked with our vital organs exposed. We were now more susceptible to predators. Big brains meant premature, helpless babies. Nature selected for those who pair bonded. Love became a tool necessary for our survival. If you are one of those people looking for the point of the exercise, it's in there somewhere... I know it. As a species, we now blow away our expected life span and after a certain amount of time in a pair bond it might start to feel . . . natural.

Man: So she wonders to herself: Is this it? Are the sacrifices that have been made for life to continue worth it? If love is simply another adaptation, how does she use this information to assess her status as a pair-bonded animal. Is she satisfied with it?

Lucy: Well that's the question, right? After the match has been struck, it's intense and then a slow, steady burn. Is it possible that's the pay off? Is the line between stability and drudgery so fine that we often miss it?

Man: Perhaps, she thinks to herself, that it is truly better to have felt the passion than to live a lifetime without feeling its intensity.

Lucy: Perhaps people venture down this road without knowing the things we are signing ourselves up for. If love, passionate love, is the gift of flight, (She pauses and considers the gravity of her question.) . . . is marriage is a cage?

Man: Maybe there is no payoff. Perhaps it is all so subtle. We continue to live, pair bond, adapt, love, marry and all of this stability makes us happy.

(Lucy holds up the shirt to inspect.)

Lucy: Maybe we are happy, truly happy. But we just don't know it.

(The man winces at the thought of this being a true statement. Lucy shrugs apologetically to him. He stares to the floor ahead of him and nods, knowingly. He crosses to her side of the stage.)

Man: I have to get to work, sweets. I'm late.

(He gives her a platonic, yet tender kiss on the forehead).

Lucy: All right. Home by dinner, right? Taco night!

(The man exits stage left and Lucy continues to iron, contentedly.)

Miah Sommer resides in Omaha, Nebraska with his wife, Katie, their sons Henry and Charlie, and their dog, Willie. Sommer studied History and Religion at the University of Nebraska Omaha. He is the Executive Director and Founder of The Bike Union Mentoring Project, a social enterprise that serves at-risk youth.

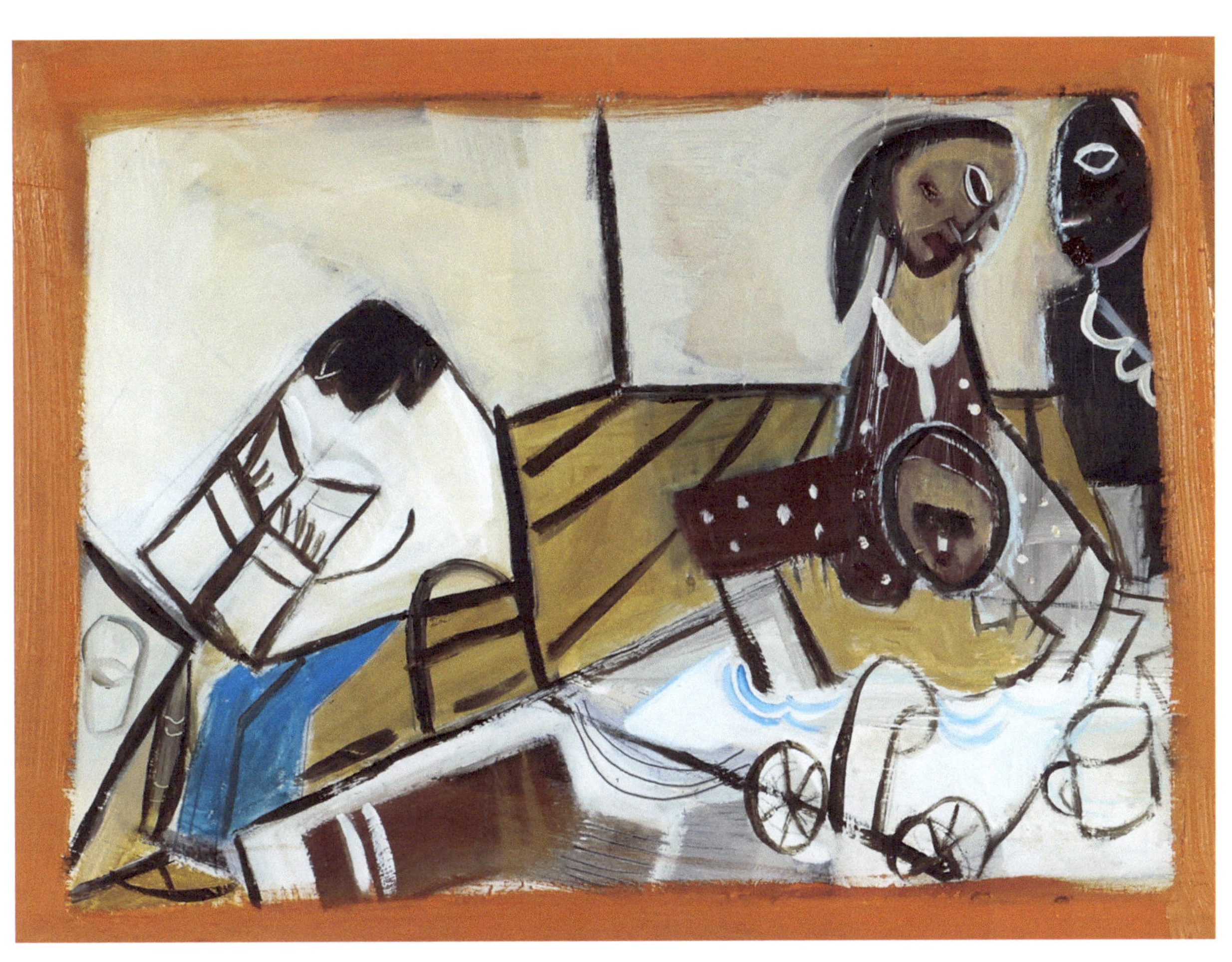

Will You Please Wash Me, Please? | Joe Hoover

"When he was in college my brother Frankie used to carry his books around campus in a mailbox. Did you know that Poppy?"

Poppy smiled and slapped at the water.

"We all just said that's who he is. No one thought anything of it. Dorothy, can you get me the Brillo pad?"

"Where is it?"

"Where does anyone keep Brillo pads? Lord."

Mary plunged her hands in the water again.

"But I thought about it a couple of days ago. Why did he carry his books in a mailbox? And why didn't we confront him about it?"

"You haven't given me a lot of information about how to find the Brillo."

"The least he could have done was use a shoeshine box. That would have been understandable. A jewelry box. I would have gone to Goodrich and found him a milk crate. But a mailbox? Maybe it was a cry for help."

"Maybe it was a cry for mail."

"Have you got that scouring pad? This child's getting dirtier every minute with your dawdling."

"Don't use those nasty words on me. Dawdling. I haven't dawdled in I don't know how long. Besides, I'm the best maid you ever had."

"What are you talking about?"

"You mean I'm not the best?"

"You're not my maid at all. You're my neighbor. You work at Mutual. You just came over to borrow something."

"Well."

"What did you want this time? Heroin?"

"Iron. Your iron."

"Oh. That's easier to get."

"If I were his daddy I would have told that boy we're not paying for him to go around college looking like a bird."

Outside the sky hung low over the city. It was the gray color of despair. Weeks-old snow covered the ground with a beauty that was not obvious to anyone. The snow was tamped-down and sand-flecked. The snow was vaguely hurtful. Inside the furniture had been moved out and the wood floor waxed clean. They were all breathing in wax fumes and no one seemed to mind. They couldn't care less. Hope had left their home. Hope was gone, plain gone. She'd left earlier that morning to hit the slopes at NebraSKI, leaving Pop Warner with Mary. Mary didn't mind the least bit. Her sister Hope was not some irresponsible teen mother. She was twenty-two. She was twenty-two and in fact gloriously irresponsible, obsessed with showing the world you could slalom on the Plains.

"A bird?"

"Birds always make nests in mailboxes. He was carrying his nest around."

"I have never thought of it that way. His nest. His home." Mary wiped her hands on her well-worn brown dress, a dress that looked as if she even slept in it, but carefully. "He was like a homeless man carrying his box around."

"You gotta read behind the lines Mary. Read behind the lines. I'm good at that." Dorothy looked around the room meaningfully. "Really good. I can read behind anybody's lines."

The hens in the building courtyard made their usual racket. Mary looked out the window and smiled. The Czarneickis were not part of that early millennium trend of chickens roaming city backyards. Mary's parents had owned hens for years. The five children fought over who would collect each morning. All of South Omaha came for the fresh eggs. Mary and Lon kept up the tradition in their own place. They grew so fond of the hens they even let them wander through the apartment. This was why nearly all the furniture was removed, the pictures taken down, the kitchen floor mopped and waxed for the fourth time that week and Pop Warner having played in the chickens**t (in front of him they always pronounced it with asterisks) was being scrubbed with a Brillo pad, if people could ever find it.

"Will you look at Poppy? He's getting so big. We won't have room in this tiny apartment for him and Lonny and Hope and me and you always barging in. For the love of God, we wash this child in the kitchen sink! Things are desperate, like that sky outside. How are we going to make ends meet? Christmas is right around the corner and we'll have nothing for this family. Not a thing."

"What are you talking about? You have a bathtub, it's just filled with furniture. There's two other bedrooms you don't even use. Lonny over there makes plenty of money teaching prose-poetry at Metro. You do Pilates at a fancy gym twice a day sometimes."

"Well."

"Why they named a lady exercise after that old fool I never will understand."

Poppy started splashing in the sink.

"See. He knows. Splashing in there like it was holy water to keep that skirted Roman devil away."

Water splashed onto Mary's brown dress, the dress she had on all the time. It was a contentious garment that had been born again, you might say, and Mary now wore it for all it was worth. Mary's mother Mother (truly, this was her name from birth) purchased it with typing money years ago at Brandeis. It was Mother's favorite dress. She gave it to her daughter to wear on her wedding day. Mary knew the offering of the dress was a sly and venomous dare. She lived with Lonny before they were married. If you weren't ashamed to do that, Mother was saying through the intermediary of dyed pima, then you shouldn't be ashamed to wear this. A brown spotted dress on your wedding day. In Mary's imagination Mother said this with teeth clenched, emphasizing in particular the "sh" and "th" sounds.

Mary almost did wear it. She even had it on three hours before the wedding, in a smiling carefree way that merely capped the molten spite surging through her new Pilates-flattened stomach. In the end she wore an ivory gown but kissed Lon at the altar much longer than a normal wedding couple might and hoped that her mother would get the message. (What exactly that message was, Mary would not have been able to say.)

Aside from her matrimonial fury Mary had to admit she respected her mother, in a Montgomery vs. Rommel kind of way. Mother was a worthy opponent who marshaled limited but potent resources to fight for an end she believed in passionately. This was worthy of deference.

It was several months before Mary and Mother finally reconciled. It happened over enchiladas molé down on 24th Street, where they both commented that if the Mexicans (with humble beauty and grace) could once and for all take over South Omaha from the Poles, they too could vanquish their own divisions.

Absently washing Pop Warner's rubbery feet as he churned up waves in the sink, Mary wondered if shame somehow had driven Frankie to his mailbox. The shame that long ago was poured down on the Czarneickis like a deluge of gutter water. That fell not just upon wedding dresses but smothered laughter and tears and all overt displays of emotion; that upbraided religious laxity and unholy moments of taking pleasure in life. The obvious culprits for all of this was Mother, or even father, but they might simply have been vessels. Shame could have come through their parents' own mothers and fathers. Shame may just as well have blown in from the unforgiving Plains out west or seeped in from South Omaha itself and the guilty decades of executing cows.

All the kids lived with shame - except Hope of course, to whom nothing could stick. Not even having a baby outside of marriage. If you judged Hope for this or for anything, that was your problem, as she strapped skis on top of her Peugeot and blistered down the road. Frankie had no such constitution. Everything stuck to him. Even other people's hurts. He lived six blocks away from Mary and Lon but never came over. He just sat at home or shuffled solitary around town as if he was bearing in his heart the pain of the world, or needed new Docs, or both.

Mary felt her own shame was vanishing bit by bit every time she washed chickens**t off her nephew.

"It's pill-AH-tees. He was German."

Dorothy brought over the scouring pad. She found it in a plant hanging wearily over charred recipe books. "He was probably named after that coward and switched the pronunciation. You're gonna ruin that baby's skin with this thing. He's not a burned pan."

"Are you his mother?"

"Are you?"

Mary took the Brillo to his neck, gently.

"Speaking of mothers, how's Devon?"

"We did our best with that child. And there he is, just another young black man in jail. This world."

"What are you talking about? He's not in jail. He's never done a wrong thing in his life. He has a good job as a draftsman."

"In Papillion. You ever been to Papillion? Office has these scraggy bushes out front. His cubicle's the size of Monet's Haystacks hanging in my parlor. The size of the picture, not the haystacks. Not the man's finest work, though many say so. But it does bring me a bit of peace nonetheless. Life grinds you down. And no, I didn't sleep with your husband."

The room went dead silent. Mary dropped the sponge in the sink. Lonny, who had never wheeled around in his thirty-eight years of life, wheeled around. Even the baby stopped splashing and looked up at Dorothy, staring with an eerie calm. Mary finally spoke, her words chosen very carefully, a child in a spelling bee articulating letters with hope and rage. "I never asked if you slept with my husband."

"Not in so many words. But I know. I told you I can read behind the lines. It's all over this place like Murphy's Oil. Saying I dawdle. I dawdle? You might as well have accused me outright. Just because I had that crazy week with Terry's cousin Terry. That was an aberration. It wasn't me. That was some other morally wayward mixed-up woman dawdling where she pleased."

"Is that what this is about? Oh Dorothy. Dorothy. Honey, we went over that six years ago. It was a terrible time. Banks were collapsing. Homes were lost. The president was white. Bread lines were everywhere. Gaunt men in felt hats and rough cotton shirts started riding the rails and learning harmonica. No one knew which way was up."

"I don't recall all those things. But I do know I was lost."

"Besides, if Lon ever did something like that I'd be onto it within the hour. I can smell shame ten miles away. I didn't suspect you of anything."

From the table there was a long exhale.

"For a second I was wondering if I did do it and just forgot." Lon shook his head and laughed. "Can you imagine doing a thing like that, with that fire cracker over there, and not remembering?"

"Okay Lon."

"I mean, how could you forget a steamy night of forbidden--"

"We get the idea Lon."

"You weren't setting me up to tell me what a terrible home-wrecking woman I was?"

"No, dear. Not at all."

Dorothy's eyes shone. "Who's the fool now?"

"No one. You've been beating yourself up for years over that week with the other Terry. It's time to let it go. We love you. Our casa is your casa. In fact, do me a favor, and bring up our little darlings from the courtyard. Kids today don't get enough germs.

"And Dorothy? The iron's in the bathtub."

Dorothy smiled at Mary. "You're the best." Mary looked down and fished out the Brillo. Lon wheeled back around to the table. Pop Warner raised his arms as if he was signaling some kind of joyous and water-soaked touchdown.

And outside the city glowed like a thousand low-wattage night-lights. The birds had gone silent. The telephone wires hummed. The snow got colder, if that was possible. People walked around as if nothing happened. As if there was no shame and no confusion. No bridal wear to reclaim and nothing afoot that might bring them to the crumbling edges of hell itself. As if they weren't being saved every minute by four unlikely angels working out their destinies in a stripped-down second-floor apartment. In the distance a Peugeot fishtailed down the street, heading home.

“What are you mumbling over there Lon? That is about the craziest prose-poem you have ever come up with.”

“I didn’t think it was so --

“Come on. Let’s put these pictures back up and call Frankie over. Get the baby dirty and let him wash it.”

Joe Hoover is a writer, actor, and a Jesuit brother who also teaches at St. Ignatius grammar school in New York City. His essays have been published in AGNI, The Sun, *and* The Best Spiritual Writing 2012. *"Occupy My Heart" was selected as a Notable Essay in* Best American Essays 2013. *Joe is poetry editor at* America Magazine.

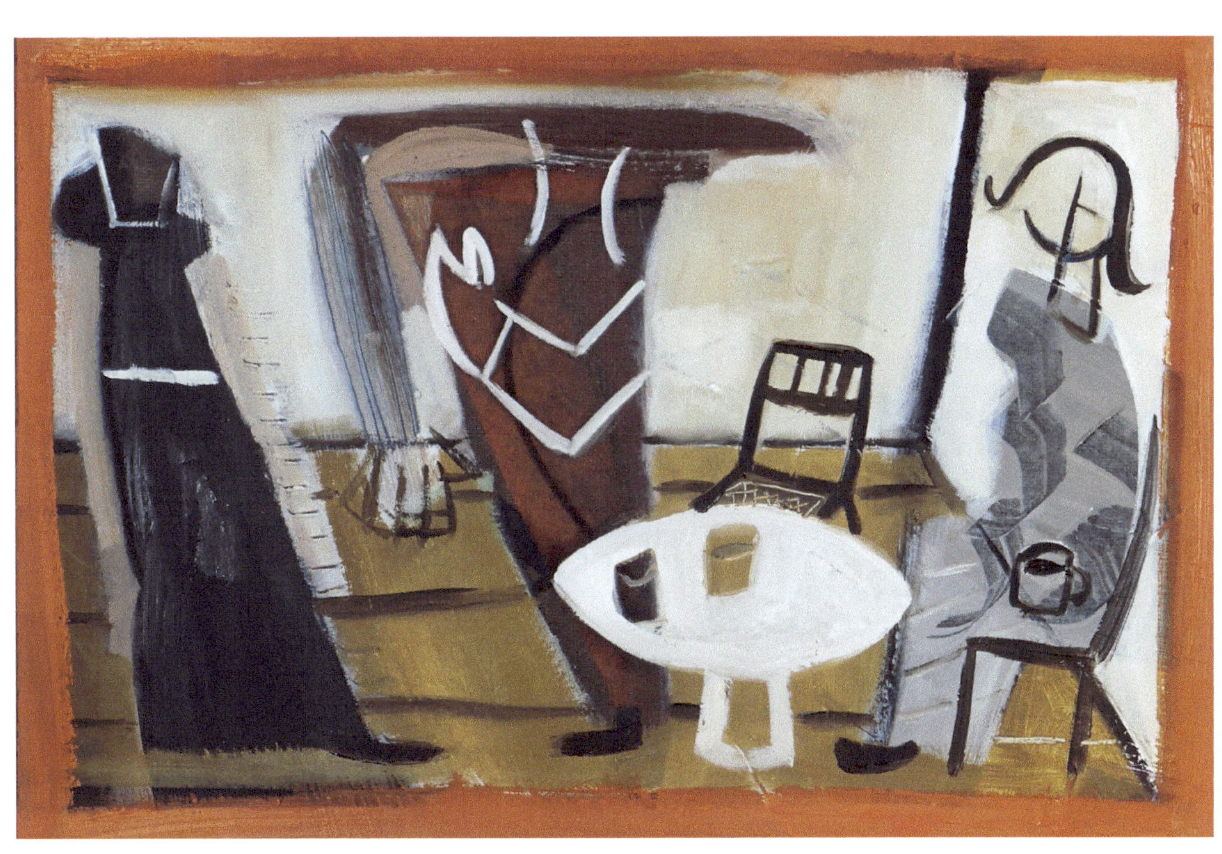

Roommates | Matt Mason

The Fog, Pumpkin Pie, and the other roommate found this to be an ideal arrangement.

Sure, it was cramped and, you know, damp, a little messy, but the three were relieved to find roommates who, well, worked. Being an archetype, you see, isn't all ambrosia and golden apple; in fact, it tends to piss off your average Joe.

Imagine, for instance, you move into an apartment and find out you're rooming with The Fog. Hey, it might seem magical at first, maybe even for a while, what, with the silver of that mist in morning light. But what about after a week of your damp clothes, the way your hair frizzes into a tower of rat-nest, the complete lack of dry bread and, inevitably, all the mold? Normal people can't put up with this. You wouldn't be able to put up with this.

And that's just The Fog, who's otherwise quite wonderful. I don't think I need to go into Pumpkin Pie, and I know I don't need to mention how long anyone would last with the other.

Despite their disparate schedules, the three gathered for tea almost every morning. Pumpkin Pie, ever the pleasing host, would make it from his impressive collection of flavors. The Fog always had more shine on licorice mornings, and the other, of course, gravitated toward black: no cream, no sugar, no nothing, black. Pumpkin Pie, of course, didn't care what flavor, as there inevitably wasn't much tea in his cup, more a cream and sugar soup with a few dollops of tea-flavor.

When the other wasn't there for tea, Pumpkin Pie and The Fog learned they should not turn on the radio that day.

One morning, The Fog surprised everyone. She went down to the bakery on 40th Street and brought back a box of fresh cinnamon rolls. As soon as the lid opened, Pumpkin Pie went pale and backed against the wall. He'd grown up with them; Steve, Mona, and Ole were some of his closest friends in the old neighborhood. This was the first time The Fog ever saw the other smile.

Matt Mason has won a Pushcart Prize and two Nebraska Book Awards; was a finalist for the position of Nebraska State Poet; organized and conducted poetry programming with the U.S. Department of State in Nepal, Botswana, Belarus, and Romania; and has been on six teams at the National Poetry Slam.

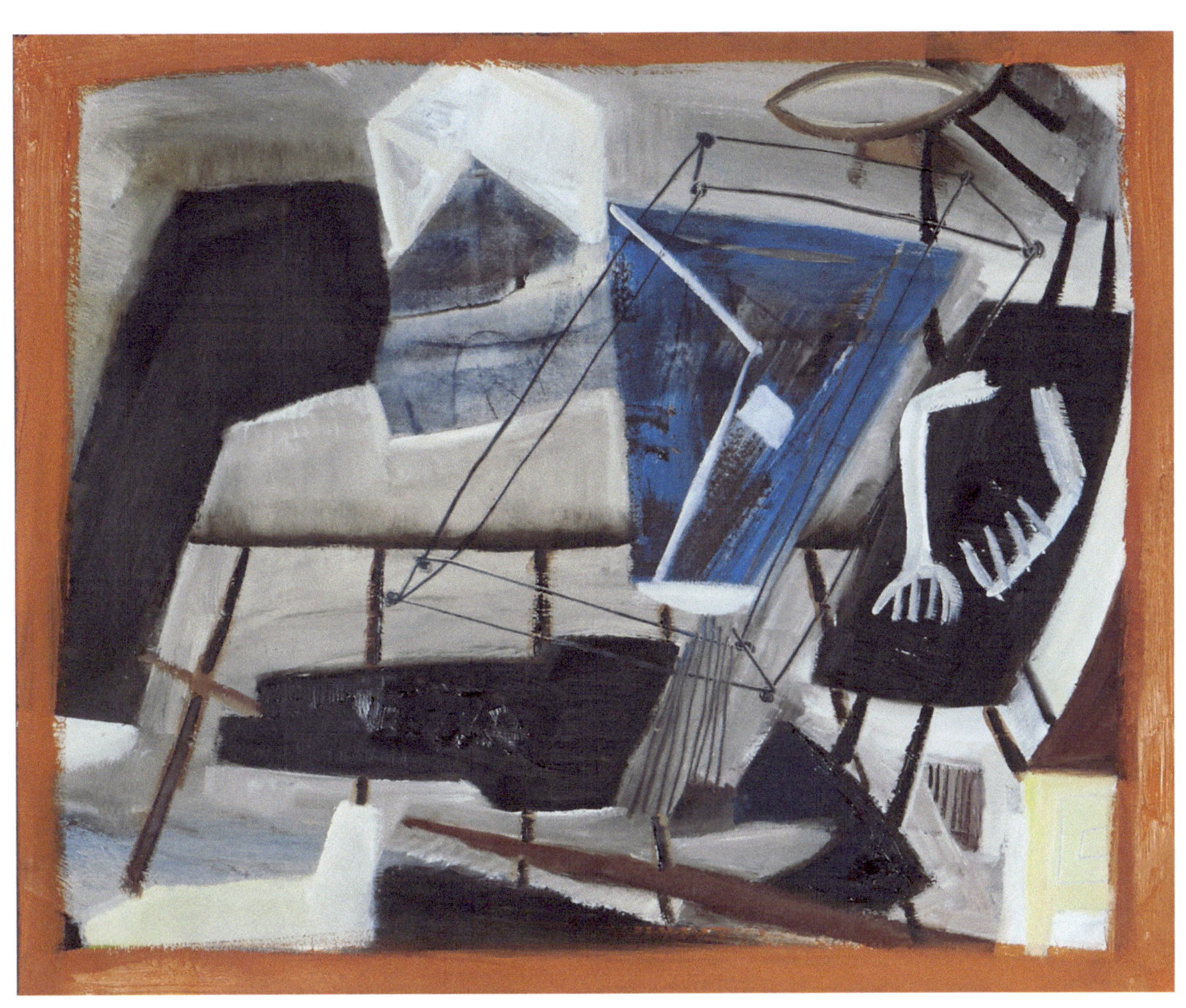

Little Things I Know | Todd Robinson

Seventy percent chance of rain today—that's a free shower
for the dirty Kia across the street. Here's a dumb secret
I just figured out: everybody chose silver paint to escape
expensive car washes. It doesn't show dirt. That's the point.
Here's another little thing I know: there's a motherfucking dog
growling behind every sinner's chain-link fence, damaging

the grass because we're lonely monkeys. Life damages.
My wife says we're more apish than monkeys, showering
the window planters with tap water. We've never had a dog
or a baby, because like that. I keep too many secrets,
have a hankering for booze, don't see any fucking point.
After work today we're going to get blitzed, escape

the echo chambers of our brainpans. The work of escaping
this gritty apartment is fun. It's all a little more damaged
when we come to, the knives in gray water more pointed,
the unfolded laundry, the ragged rugs, the scummy shower
all we can see, but every life hides behind a secretive
door. Unleash the hounds of Saturday and get dogged

about spring cleaning, work like a serf until the last dogs
die and you can sleep in the quiet hum of clean escapism:
when your surfaces are spotless, you know the secret.
When I was a high-school malcontent I read a damaged
paperback edition of *Steppenwolf.* In the gym's showers
Germany gleamed in my eyes: a foyer, the rounded point

of a broom, a *hausfrau* engaging with her pointless
day: sweep and mop and scrub the world, tired as a dog
but proud as a parrot. I guess you can't say shower
and Germany in the same sentence anymore. Escaping
history isn't easy. But with a little brain damage,
self-administered, you'll forget, and learn new secrets.

I sit on this stoop with my booze, my smoke, my secrets,
the missus going in and out the place like there's a point
to this or any afternoon. I just want to get damaged

and covet the neighbor's wife with the hot little dog,
tilt my neck to receive cold cans of American escape,
maybe get a little sunburned in the sun-shower.

I'd give my left tit for the secrets of a barking dog—
it cares not if the point is making puppies or just escape
from a car wheel's damage. Peace in any rain shower.

Todd Robinson teaches in the Writer's Workshop at University of Nebraska Omaha. Most recently, his work has appeared in Arc Poetry Review, burntdistrict, Chiron Review, *and* Sugar House Review. *He has known Bill since 1991.*

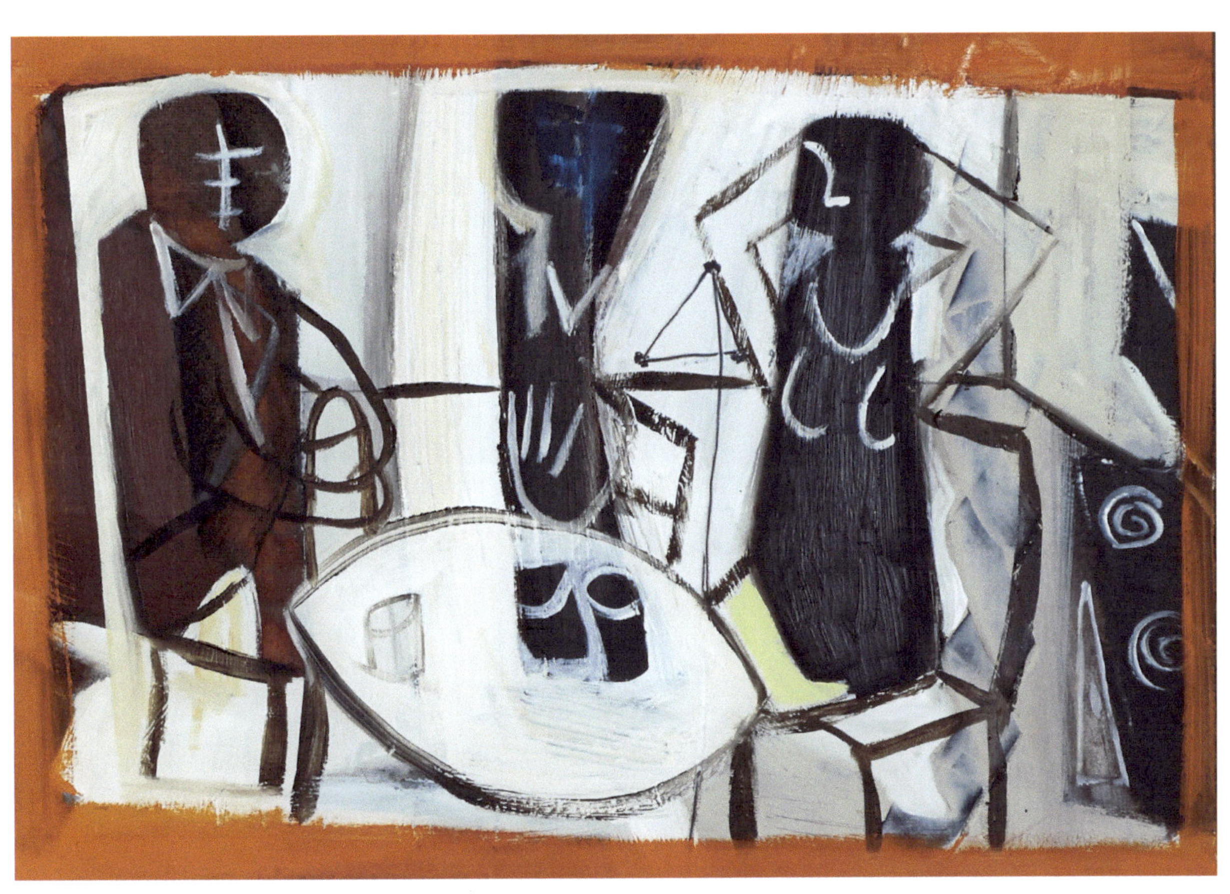

Mites | Dan McCarthy

"Did I tell you guys I thought I had bedbugs?" said Eric.

Becca lifted her feet a centimeter off the floor.

Nicole had been sitting with her fingers woven behind her head, a novel posture in her third trimester. She stayed like that and said: "So what makes you think you don't have bedbugs, if you thought you did?"

"Well, the main thing is that I'm not getting bit anymore. And I don't think — I'm 99 percent sure — I never had bedbugs in the first place."

"Okay, but why did you think you had them?" said Nicole.

"Because I was getting bit, at night, in bed. So, bedbugs, right? And I had just been down in Missouri at that ragtime fest with Andrew, and we stayed in that old hotel."

Andrew was the downstairs neighbor, a piano player who was always practicing old-timey party music. You could hear him, very well, through the floor.

"And so, of course, I'm looking online at all these pictures of bedbug bites and stories about bedbug infestations. My bites looked a little different, and where they were on my body isn't usually where bedbugs bite."

"Where were you getting bitten?" said Becca. She was trying to be nice and smile, so she wore a look of smiling disgust.

"It was, um, in my swimsuit area."

Nicole took a sip of coffee to hide her grin. Becca squinted for more information.

"Usually bedbugs bite you where your skin is exposed while you're asleep, and I was getting bit under my underwear. I wear underwear to bed."

Now Becca smiled for real.

"And it would hurt like hell when they bit me, it would wake me up, but then it wasn't itchy for very long, and the bites didn't look like bedbugs, and plus I was inspecting my mattress and sheets and everything and couldn't find any traces. So, thank you Internet, I came to the conclusion that they were bird mites."

Mites are parasites so tiny they can be invisible, he said. The nastiest itchy shit you hear about is caused by mites: scabies, chiggers, mange. Words that sound older than medicine. Dust mites, for example, are human parasites, but they only eat dead human cells, like your skin after it flakes off of you. Get this: there is a kind of mite that only lives at the base of the human eyelash. That's its whole universe, your eyelashes.

"But bird mites can't live on humans — they're not parasites for humans; they can only live on birds."

"Wait, they bite you — they eat you in your sleep — but they can't live on you?" said Nicole.

"Yeah, it's like if you were starving and went out and ate some grass. You couldn't survive on it."

"So if you can't see them, what makes you sure you had bird mites?" Becca was only now letting her feet rest on the floor.

"The main, like, diagnosis for bird mites is if there are birds' nests on your building. When the birds leave the nest, the mites go looking for a new host. And there can be millions of mites living in a nest."

"And there were nests on your building?" said Becca.

"Yeah, this spring there were some house finches that built a nest up under the roof of my deck out there. Real cute. Kind of like a sparrow but with a reddish head. There was a male and a female and they had four chicks. Like an adorable nature program, except then it turns out there are millions of parasites all over them. And when the chicks left the nest last week, I started getting these bites."

"So is the nest still up there?" Becca was imagining microscopic insects crawling over her shoes. She thought about tucking her pants into her socks.

"No, I knocked it down a few days ago, once I figured out that that was probably what was biting me. I was so grossed out, I put on gloves and a face mask and took a broom and knocked the nest down, and then I sprayed it with some spray I got at the hardware store. I probably looked totally nuts, going hazmat on this little birds' nest."

"Well it's good you figured it out," said Nicole.

"Yeah, I still haven't been going out there to smoke though. I go clear out front. I'm afraid there's still some survivors crawling around." Eric got up to pour some more coffee. "It kind of makes you crazy."

Upstairs, in the apartment above, the baby was crying and nobody could see what was the matter.

Dan McCarthy is a songwriter and piano player living in Omaha, Nebraska. He first got to know Bill Hoover when they were both playing rhythm banjo in an old-time string band called the Short Timers.

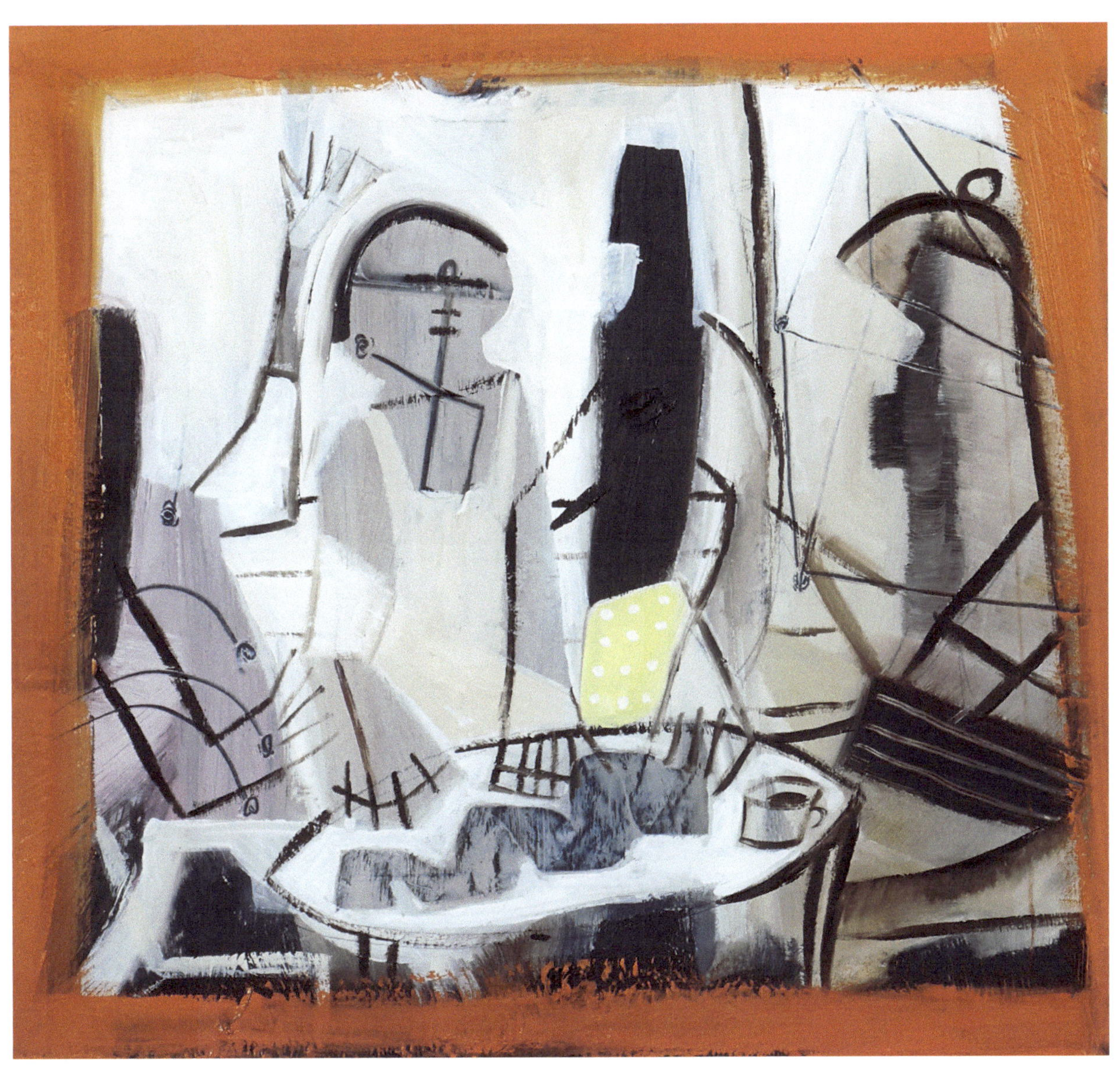

Wax and Wane | Amy Shearn

Alexa Sturm, the oppressively friendly new girl in 2B, had invited Lily for coffee the maximum amount of times allowable to refuse, which, technically speaking, is five. Five times Lily conjured excuses almost immediately, lies spewing from her lips with an alacrity that alarmed her: she wasn't feeling well (that one was easy, as she was almost never feeling well lately); she was slammed with work; a needy friend had come to town; she needed to go across town to return a cable box; her niece had given her lice. With the tale of nits she realized she was already starting to sound like a liar. No one was five-refusals busy. Also, she lacked a niece, which made it a complicated story to keep up with.

The sixth time she was caught off guard, near the grid of mailboxes in the lobby, nervous at being seen checking mail so many hours before the mailman arrived. She had cocked her head in a way that Alexa read as a nod, and before she knew it, Lily was sitting in the cluttered kitchen of 2B, assaulted by hipster-antique-mall knick-knacks, a cup of muddy percolated coffee steaming before her.

None of this was surprising. Lily had misunderstood and been misunderstood frequently in the past few days. A confluence of sebaceous exuberance and mild self-neglect had resulted in her left ear becoming completely plugged with wax. It was a condition so horrifying Lily had a hard time admitting to herself that it was in fact the case. For a day or two she thought hopefully that she might be going deaf. At least deafness had some gravitas, a promise of a different life. The plugged ear only made her feel off-balance and easily confused. "What? What?" she had said for three days straight.

Unfortunately, this was the kind of thing Lily was prone to ignore. She still had not made a doctor's appointment. Her new nightly routine involved bathing her ear in a repellent vinegar mixture that made her gag. She did this to herself, as she lived alone.

Since Alexa had moved into the building in July, Lily had never officially met her boyfriend, but knew from hallway encounters, expert eavesdropping, and the evidence that now surrounded her – photo strips stuck to the fridge, framed gig posters – that a boyfriend did live there with her: an enormous black man who played clarinet in a kind of band Lily couldn't quite get the gist of, no matter how many times Alexa explained it. What was conceptual jazz anyway? Lily imagined a smoky room full of people sitting in silence, conceptualizing jazz.

Alexa herself was tiny, kinetic, whiter than Lily herself. Lily had known it was merely a matter of time before Alexa sought her out, by simple virtue of Lily being one of the only other white 30-somethings in the building – if you didn't count the handful of young families who lived a reality and schedule all their own, which of course she didn't.

Alexa (Lily knew within a few sips of coffee) had moved to the city for Alfred's music concept and had yet to find a job, which explained her rabid enthusiasm for the coffee-time company of Lily, who, even Lily could admit to herself, was a somewhat pallid conversationalist. Her husband had mentioned this once the whiff of divorce was in the air and everything else was being aired along with it. Couldn't Lily ask him a damn question for once? Couldn't Lily think of anything interesting to say, ever? Did Lily really think people were satisfied for her to sit there, smiling and nodding, a bobblehead of perpetual agreement? Lily didn't bother to mention that until recently he himself had seemed to enjoy this about her. There was no point in saying this to him. He hated being disagreed with.

"I actually just got back into town from my first visit home since we moved here!" Alexa cried, as if this were the most fascinating detail imaginable. Lily placed a bet with herself: South Dakota, and a youth spent in Midwestern theatre which had been sublimated, in deference to the husband's career and a lack of potential, in equal measure. "Good old Wisconsin," said Alexa, waving her hands as she tended to whenever she spoke. Lily gave herself partial credit.

"Wisconsin! I'm from Michigan!" From her vantage point behind the plugged ear, Lily's voice sounded submerged.

Alexa presented jazz hands of happiness.

"I actually was recently home, too," Lily added in what she hoped was a normal volume.

Alexa explained that even though they'd spent every cent moving here and surviving these past few months, she'd had to fly home because her grandmother had died.

Lily put down her coffee and leaned forward, uncertain she'd heard properly. "Your grandmother?" Yes, Alexa confirmed, the grandmother had died at age 100 exactly. Lily shook her head. "That's so weird. I mean, I'm sorry. But also, my grandmother just died. At age 100 exactly. That's why I was back in Michigan last week."

Alexa, too, had traveled the previous week. They had both seen their younger brothers whom they had not seen in years and barely related to, so weirdly successful had the brothers become in related fields of finance. They had both visited influential, beloved, male high school teachers who now struck them as kind of molesty. They had both encountered old boyfriends they'd never really gotten over. They had both been running late to the airport for the return flight.

Alexa's arms flailed like a preacher at a revival. "You are kidding!" she screamed with every likeness.

Lily shook her head unhappily. "No."

“You know what else is weird?” Alexa said, pouring more coffee. Lily would never get out of there. She looked mournfully at the coffee pot the size of a gallon jug. She was a grown woman, a woman who had been through a divorce no less. She should have learned by now how to protect herself from people. But the plugged ear made her feel more dull and stupid than usual, and it was difficult to strategize. No sudden moves. Alexa said, “I was going to mention this before – but my middle name is Lily.”

Lily blinked. It was awful. You thought you were a person. You thought you were you. And then an idiotic extrovert from the second floor dragged you down into ordinariness. The worst of it was, Lily’s middle name was Alexandria, close enough. But she wouldn’t tell her this; wouldn’t give Alexa the idea that they were soul sisters, or different faces of the same coin, or whatever they were. Alexa seemed silly enough to read divinity into coincidence, a fallacious thought process Lily hadn’t engaged in since junior high.

“Isn’t this all too amazing!” Alexa cried.

Lily tilted her head like a dog listening for a leash jingle. Something moved in her ear. The nature of the wax made it easier for her to hear Alexa than her own voice, a very unsettling situation to find herself in. But then a liquidy gurgle offered an inkling of relief.

She had been sad that her grandmother died, and surprised that she was sad, and sad or maybe surprised to learn that you didn’t need to be surprised by something in order to be saddened by it. See also: her divorce, finalized in July. Home for the funeral – she’d said she couldn’t miss more than a few days of work, as if the HR department she worked for couldn’t be entirely run by a computer and a temp, which of course it could and probably soon enough would be – Lily had gone for long walks in her parents’ suburban neighborhood the likes of which she hadn’t taken since age 11 or so. She stopped for a long time at the playground at the end of the subdivision. She’d had a vague idea of sitting on a swing and indulging in melancholy, but signs stopped her. “Do not walk on the grass. Recently seeded lawn. Establishing root structure.” Was it a haiku? It was something.

Maybe it was her. Establishing her root structure. In the city her friends were enjoying promotions, buying houses. At home there were babies everywhere she looked. The ex-boyfriend she’d run into had been taking a litter of children to the rec center where her parents belonged and she’d planned to mope on the treadmill. He’d been nice – he was always nice, that had been their problem – he’d asked after her husband. She’d said, not lying, that he was fine. He probably was fine! The ex hadn’t asked specifically if they were still married, had he?

Because she lived in the city and because she was insincerely chirpy on social media, the people back home assumed Lily’s life was characterized by glamour and adventure. Alexa referenced this now, waving her hands and pushing a plate of greasy homemade scones toward Lily’s chest: “Everyone in Wisconsin was like ‘Oh my GOD, you live in the CITY, and your husband is SO SUCCESSFUL’ and they don’t say black but they mean it and are all impressed by it in one way or another--" Lily felt herself blushing; heartbeat pulsing in the clogged ear. Were you allowed to say that? Was the black husband a trophy? Was he, like his music, conceptual? "--and you're going to have a baby; you have got it all figured out! But I'm like, um no, maybe that's how it looks, but I'm secretly terrified, how am I gonna do all this here where I don't even know anyone at all! Besides you, of course."

Lily shook her head; a bit of the wax rattled; it was excruciating. What was happening here? Had Alexa Sturm just announced she was pregnant? She didn't look pregnant, so was Lily one of the first people to be told? Was Lily being tricked into becoming Alexa's new best friend? Maybe there had been something she'd missed; some important confession that had lodged in her ear canal and become fossilized there, to be excavated by interested parties at a later date.

She stood. Alexa smiled and blinked. It's not a question of what you can do, Lily wanted to say, but what you can't not do. Except she didn't trust herself to modulate her voice into the tone that would accurately express her meaning. So instead she swallowed, gathered up her strength, said firmly, "This has been so nice, but I've just remembered something I must do."

As confidently as possible, given how off-balance she was, Lily left the apartment and strode down the hall.

Amy Shearn is the author of two novels, The Mermaid of Brooklyn and How Far Is The Ocean From Here. She is the curator/host of BOOKISH, an author interview series at the Brooklyn Public Library. She lives in a big apartment building in Brooklyn with her husband and children (and about 150 others). Visit her at amyshearnwrites.com

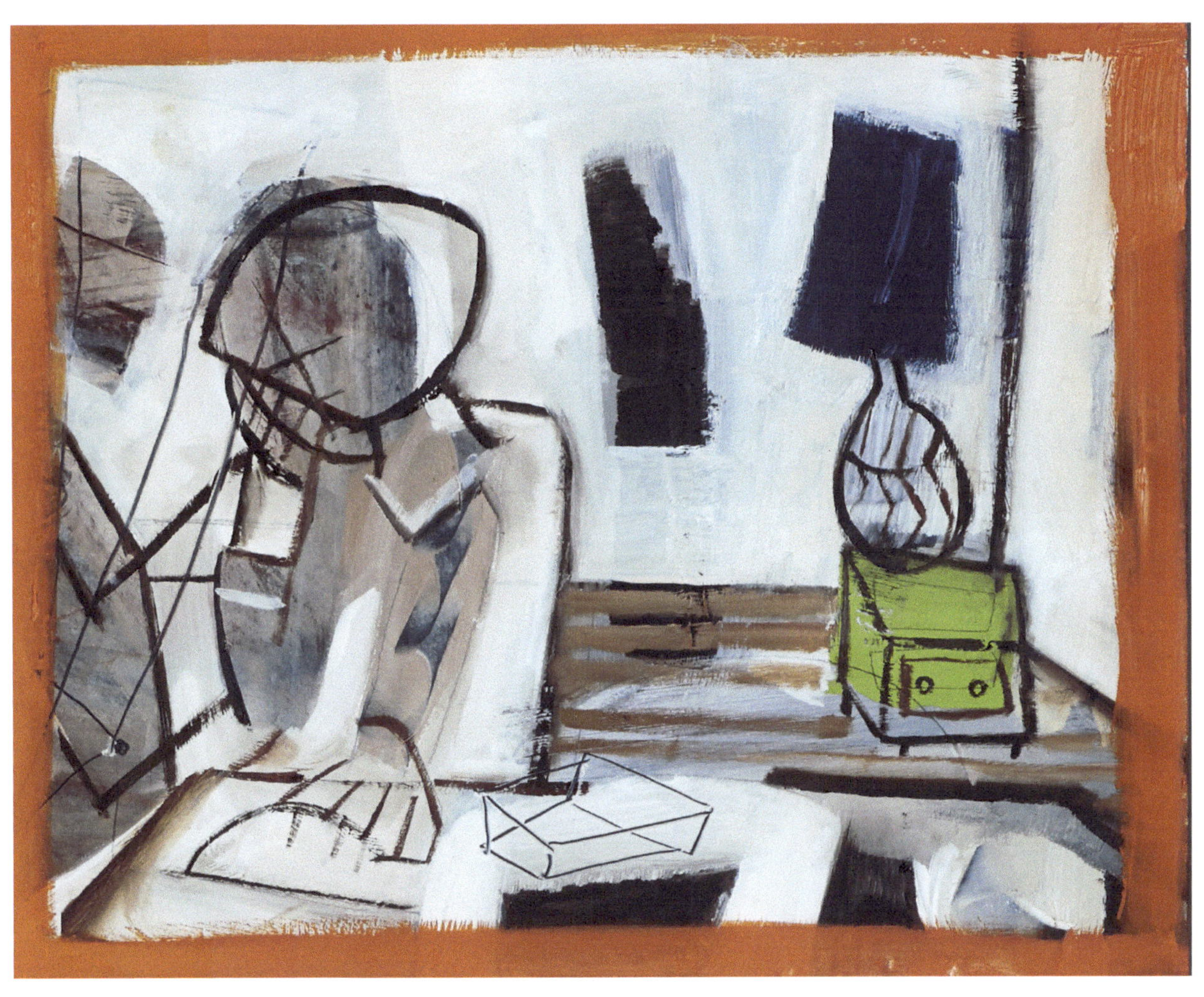

Still Life with Grieving Parents | Sarah McKinstry-Brown

Before our child became ill, the light was always changing and the kitchen was full with whatever was in season, a small mountain of apples or clementines fit to tumble from the glass bowl on the counter.

Half full, the coffee pot was sometimes left on all morning. What was the rush? The brew grew darker. The fruit ripened in tune with our appetites. Before the child became ill, all of our afters were sweet; of course she would grow up and out of our arms. Of course she would grow up and out into the world.

The child is ill and my husband doesn't remember to bring fruit home. I don't remind him. The coffee disappears almost as soon as dawn comes. I make more. I make more. I grind and measure and wait and pour. Mornings when I am alone and the child is sleeping, I stir cream and sugar into coffee, listening to the spoon clink the side of the cup.

When my husband passes behind me and stops to place his hand on my shoulder,
I know that we are so much older now. I remember the book I used to read to our girl before she got sick, "Gray Day... Everything is gray. I watch. But nothing moves today."

I tell myself that our bodies, our breaths, are just brushstrokes, and God, in his sky-blue overalls, is a painter who has put us here. I tell myself that this scene, sprung from his imagination and born of his hands, is not real. Pigment and angles and charcoal, I tell myself that our sorrow, framed by our apartment window, is nothing but light and shadow.

Winner of The Academy of American Poets Prize, Sarah McKinstry-Brown won the 2011 Nebraska Book Award for Poetry for her debut collection, Cradling Monsoons. *Sarah has been a working writer since 2002 when she sold everything she owned and went on a cross-country reading tour via the performance poetry circuit.*

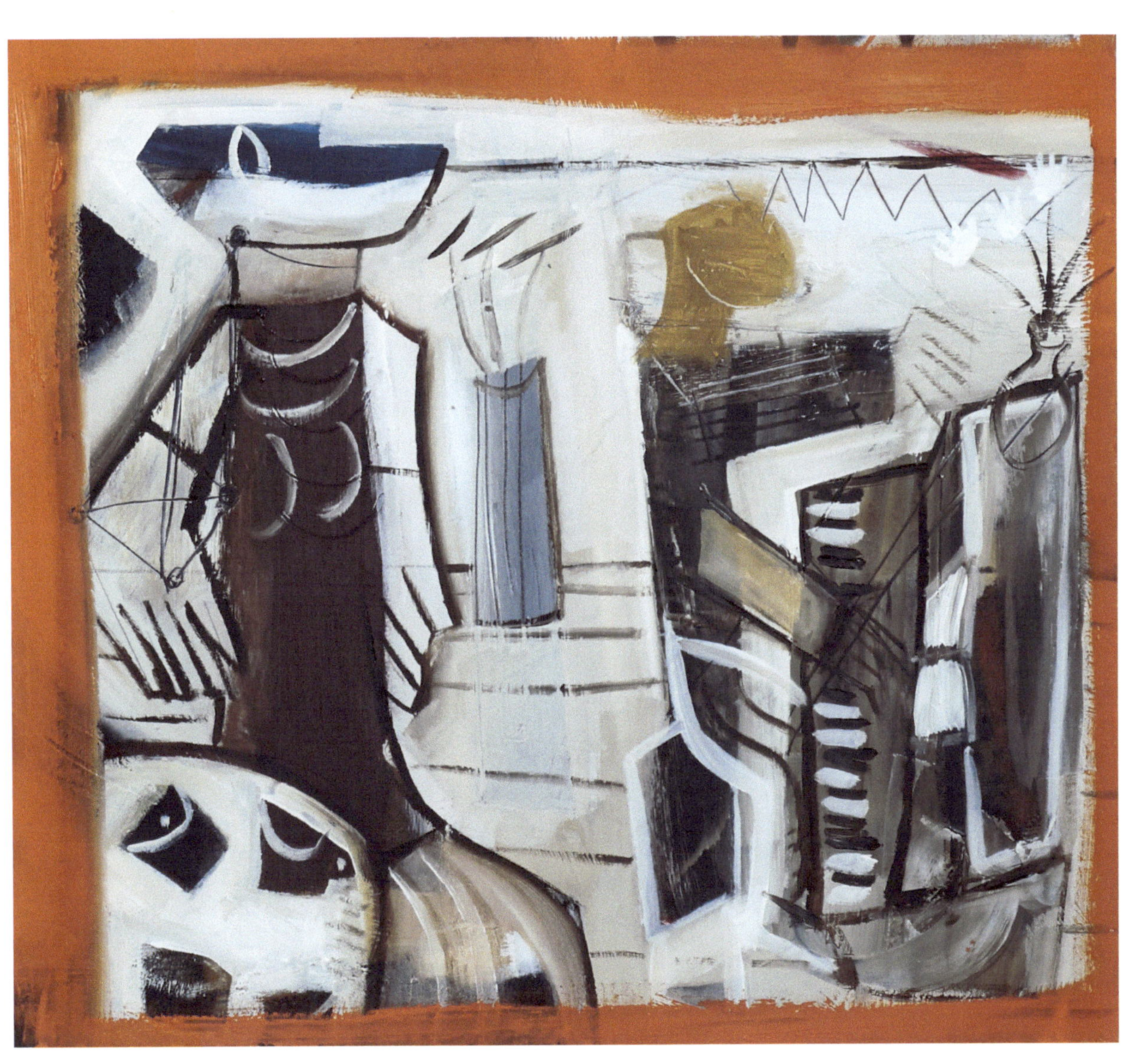

Beautiful Light | Timothy Schaffert

If you haven't yet heard the story I'm about to tell then don't read any further, or I'll spoil the end for you. It's an O. Henry story, and the end of an O. Henry is often what people like the most about it. You know, like "The Gift of the Magi," where the wife sells the locks of her long, flowing hair so she can buy her husband a fob for his beloved pocket watch, and the husband sells the beloved pocket watch so he can buy combs to decorate her long, flowing hair. That's not the story I'm telling you, though. The story I'm talking about is "The Last Leaf," the one about the starving artists in Greenwich Village. Two young women live in a drafty artist's loft, and one of the women comes down with pneumonia as winter approaches. She gets it in her head that she'll be dead when the last leaf falls from the vine on the wall she can see outside her window.

The one who's not sick tells the old man who lives in the apartment downstairs about the one that is sick, and how the sick one's counting the leaves as they fall from the vine. The old man, in the dark of night, sneaks out and paints a leaf on the wall. That last stubborn leaf never falls, and the sick one doesn't have a last leaf to count, and she starts feeling better. She lives. And it turns out that the old man – who'd always dreamed of someday painting a masterpiece – catches pneumonia out in the cold while painting the leaf, and he dies. The end.

So maybe I'll start with the end of my own story. There's a woman who's an artist and she moves into an apartment because she likes the light that comes in through the window. But she falls in love with this other woman, and this other woman is a songwriter and a singer and plays the piano. This other woman moves in and the only place her piano fits is along the wall with the windows. So out of the generosity and goodness of heart of the artist, the piano player gets to put her piano in front of the windows, blocking out the light that the artist loves. The end.

If you haven't guessed by now, I'm the first woman. The woman who's the artist. And as you can probably gather, "the end" of the story isn't really the end of the story. I don't know the end yet. I don't know how this is going to go. I love her, I do I do I do I do. I love her so much. Have I ever loved anybody the way I love Eleanor? She's in my heart, and she's in my soul. And as I sit here, listening to her play that pretty song, that beautiful, beautiful, beautiful song she wrote for me, and wrote about me, about how I'm in her heart and how I'm in her soul, it terrifies me – no, not terrifies – well, wait, yes, terrifies is what I mean – it terrifies me to think how quiet this room would be without her.

And have I ever before been someone you'd write a love song about? It's not just that she writes songs and that she loves me, but it's that my love for her has made me lovable.

"I think I almost have it," she told me when she sat me down to listen. She's made me a pot of plum-ginger tea. I think it's snowing out, out past the piano, and past the window, out into the late-winter afternoon. I think it's one of those light snowfalls that are so lovely to see, when there's no wind, and the flakes flutter and dust like soap shavings.

Eleanor's hair is chopped every other week into a handsome high-and-tight by an elderly barber down the street. I call that high-and-tight her "high-and-mighty." She goes in for the whole works – she smokes a cigar, she gets her chin slapped with cheap aftershave. She comes back a new man, and I get weak in the knees from her beauty. She smells of tobacco and black licorice. As she plays my song on her piano now, and as I watch the back of her head, I wonder what it will be like not to kiss her neck, to not whisper in her ear when I want. I wonder what it will be like when this woman I love is a stranger to me again, and I don't know where she is, or what she's doing, or who she loves.

But, you see, she only loves me some of the time. But when she does love me, she loves me like she'll die if I don't love her back. And this moment I'm having, with my love singing me the love song she wrote about our love, is unlike any love I've ever known. A person can live her whole life without ever knowing a moment like this. I'd be a fool to let this go. What is it, after all, that I expect?

And the piano had to go there in front of my window. There was simply nowhere else for it. She was supposed to leave it behind? So that I could have my light? She found that piano on the street, you know. On the street. Where she lived before, a couple were moving out of their apartment and the piano didn't fit in their moving truck, so they just left it on the sidewalk. Eleanor watched the whole thing from her apartment window, and listened – the couple contemplating the piano, weighing its value in their lives. They didn't take it at all lightly. The wife even cried, though she'd been the one to propose leaving it behind. Once they'd decided it was no longer theirs, they ran their hands over the wood. They tapped the keys. They touched at a burn scar on the lid, left by a cigarette that had been perched there, like at some blues club. They picked a splinter from the side, where it had bumped against the banister on the way out. Eleanor hoped they'd play some last song, an echo to take away with them, but they didn't. It even seemed to Eleanor that by the time they got in the truck and left, they'd already grown used to their new life without the old piano.

We left the curtains up, and we keep them closed, because what would people think when they walked by, and they looked in our window, and they saw the back of a piano? They'd think, "What kind of people are they? Who blocks out the sun like that?"

As Eleanor comes to the end of my love song, I don't care at all about the people outside. I want them to think we've boarded ourselves in and shut ourselves off. I want them to hear her piano, and her singing, and her words, and I want them to envy us our isolation.

Before I moved into this apartment, I walked by it quite often. I work just up the street, as a cocktail waitress in the lounge of an old hotel. (We serve everything in little-old-lady martini glasses, even rusty nails and shots of scotch. I can do quick-sketch caricatures, and people tip me extra if I doodle their mugs on cocktail napkins.) The people who lived here before me, their curtains were always closed too, and I often wondered what it was like inside. And when I first walked in, when it was for rent again, the place was empty and the curtains were gone, and I was instantly stunned by how the sunlight played, slipping in and out of shadows, and catching on the glass of the windowpanes and shimmering there, angel and devil both. I pictured a woman – a woman like Eleanor – sleeping naked in the light, as I painted how the sun lit her skin.

When Eleanor finishes playing my song, she stops, and she slouches, and the song still rings in my ear in the silence. Neither of us can speak. Her shoulders shake. She's crying. I fear what she'll say now that the song's over. Is her love for me too much or too little? I've heard this song before, I want to tell her, and I mostly believe it's true. On the night I first moved in, it was autumn, and the window was open, and I listened close, thinking I could hear a piano playing in the night, but it was only my ear making music of the light rain on the glass, and of the drops rattling the dry leaves of the rosebush, and the ting-ting-tap of water on the tin of the downspout.

Timothy Schaffert is the author of five novels, most recently The Swan Gondola (Riverhead/ Penguin). His work has been a pick of Barnes & Noble's Discover Great New Writers program, a New York Times Book Review Editors' Choice, and an Oprah.com Book of the Week. He is a professor of English at University of Nebraska Lincoln.

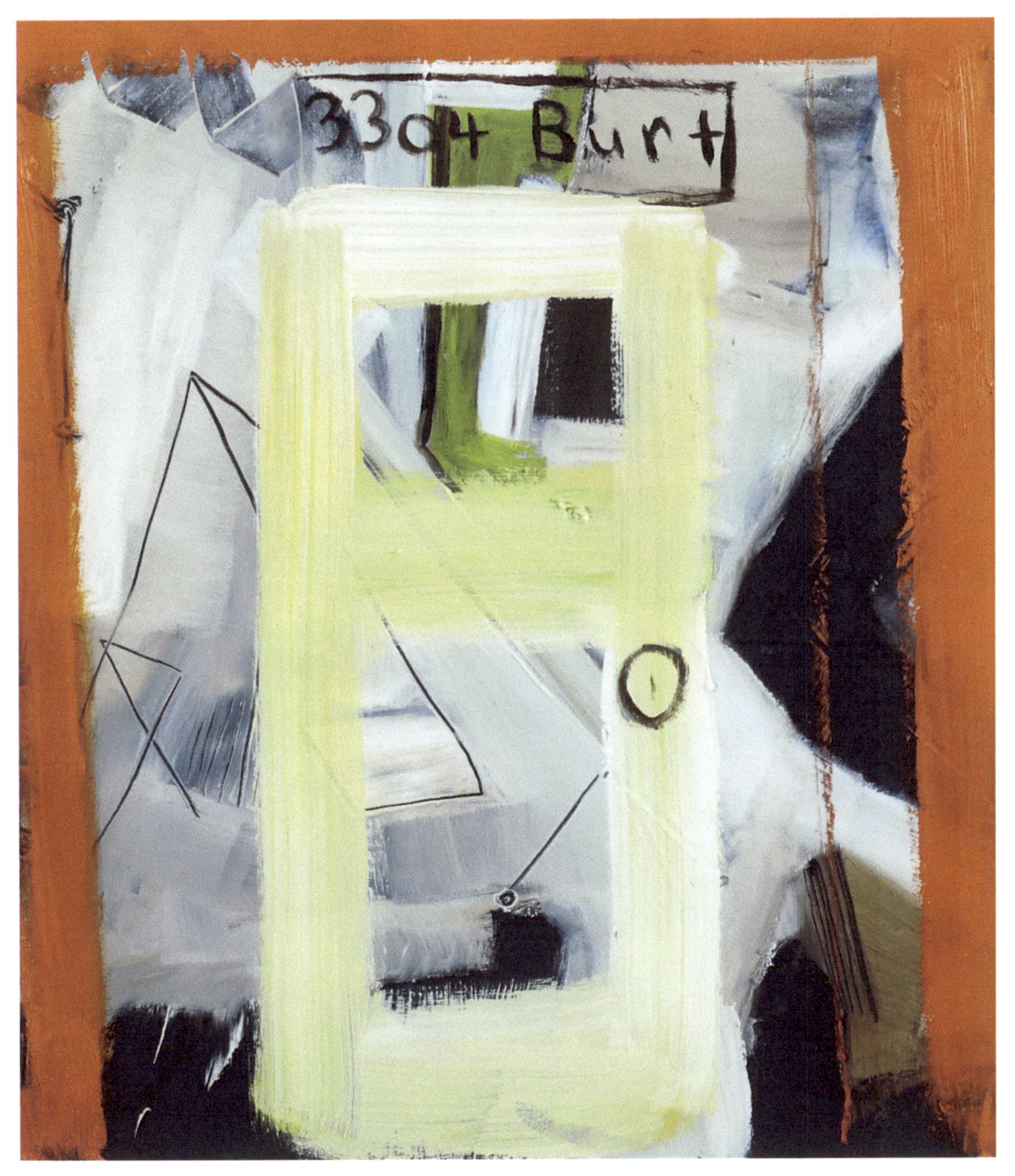
3304 Burt

Yellow Door | Kevin Lawler

Stale cigarettes
sinking jazz
broken laughter
and cabbage soup

the dark green
languor of weed
wafting past
the sunken stoop

with one bright day
after another
collapsing into
fiery years

and the dusty
windows opened
on a thousand
summer moons.

Outside on
the street
rusted cars
parked forever
with novels
smoking in
the back seat.

The mattress
on the floor
under old
wool blankets
from the
salvation store

and the sweaty
cries of sex
to briefly

set us free
from the long
slow knives
of poverty

then watching
the snow fall
while the radiators
hiss and knock
like a drunken ghost
or a steam
powered clock.

Someday this will
all be lost
under the blue
inland sea

but for now
here's the
great mouthed
golden door
swallowing lives
like a carnivore

and the painter
slowly running
up the rolling
hills of time
with yellow light
falling from his
eyes sublime.

Kevin Lawler is a poet, playwright, designer, director, producer, and actor. He is the Producing Artistic Director of the Great Plains Theatre Conference and the Artistic Director of The National Institute of the Lost. He is also a founding member of the Blue Barn Theatre. He wishes to thank his wife, daughter and geriatric poodle, Lulu, for their love and support.

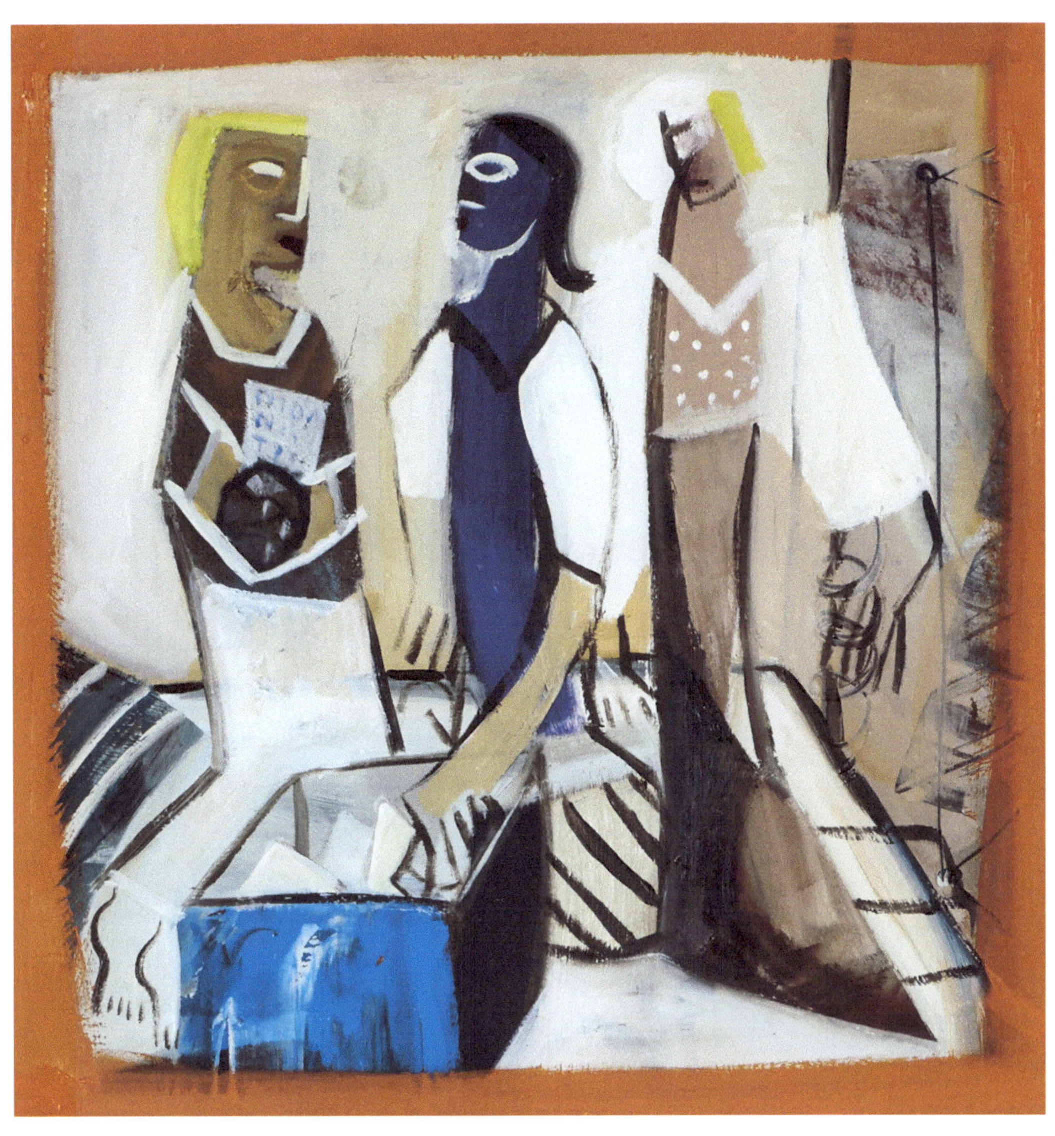

All the Ways I Am Not Sara | Rebecca Rotert

A light bulb bursts in its socket. Llewelyen clutches the front of her dress, saying, "My heavens" and then to me, "The electricity in this building. Slumlords. We will all go down in flames one day."

I unplug the lamp and remove the bulb's remains with needle-nose pliers. Replace it with a new bulb and turn the switch gingerly. I tell Llewelyn, "We should be so lucky."

My name is Molly Davies. This is Llewelyn Davies. We are the sisters in Apt. 3B. You never see us. You will never see us. We used to be three. Llewelyn, with her yellow wig, will tell you our younger sister Sara passed on long ago. I would tell you that we killed her, if you asked. But who asks two old women about their secrets? No one. Who even sees an old woman at all? Only we watch each other. And maybe Sara watches us, if you believe that sort of thing.

Here are two things a secret can do to you over time: play out in little clips like a partly remembered dream, a thing that nags at you though you have forgotten what it is or why it nags. You have over told the story with a different, better one perhaps, one that casts you in a kinder light, and now all you remember is the new version. Still, you are fearful of life's little eruptions -- a sudden burst of laughter or a shout from the apartment below, a firecracker, a sad song. Because it reminds you of the essential integrity of life in real time, before it gets interpreted, lied about, altered, re-told, renovated, improved, buried. It reminds you of the thing that is still itself under layer upon layer of cautious years. Best to avoid the world. This is how Llewelyn is with the secret.

-- or --

You put it in your shoe like a small stone and you never take it out. You wear it everywhere: to the store, the post office, to Mass. You push your weight on it day after day, step after step. It reminds you of itself as regularly as your heart beats, your breath breathes. You stand on it when someone says a kind word to you so that the kindness doesn't sink in. You let it protect the world from you in this way, a reminder of who you really are. You don't get close to anyone. You don't get close. You stand on the stone and remember Sara cuddling under your arm as a child. And look what that got her. Do not get close. This is how I am with the secret.

In short, Llewelyn's life avoids, while mine cannot forget.

As for Sara, she was beautiful. Sara was visible. A star in the firmament. A blooming magnolia. A light evening snow. A breezy ride on the streetcar in the summer. Sara was two things once: 1) Alive. 2) In love. Here she is at the small rolltop desk, her cheeks flushed, her body bent over sheets of stationary like one might a flame to protect from the wind, to encourage the vigor of fire. She is writing him. The sound of the scribbling on the soft desktop, the flush in the sound of the words being laid out for him. All that young burning love pounding into the desktop. How it enrages me. Not Llewelyn though. Here is Llewelyn giggling, teasing Sara. Here is sweet Llewelyn bringing Sara's hair around to rest on her back so that it doesn't get in the way of her writing the man she now loves. Then Sara runs across Burt Street to the mailbox without a coat on. She has enough heat in her for a dozen winters. Who needs a coat.

When his reply comes in the mail, Sara is at work. The Arcade Hotel on Douglas. This is where she met him. When his theatrical troupe passed through Omaha. I hold the letter; it vibrates unopened in my hand.

I only want to be sure. Of what? I steam the envelope. In long sentences riding up a slight invisible ramp are a kind lover's words. Only sweetness on the page but the words light up my loneliness, my ugliness, like a beacon, illuminate the terrible facts of my person, all the ways I am not Sara, will never be Sara. I'll never be seen in such a light as she. I seal the letter with a gentle brush of glue and put it in an old blue box. I watch myself do this with both eyes open. I say to myself, just this once.

Here is Sara grabbing the mailbox key every day after work and running to the boxes to check for his letters, walking up the stairs slowly, empty-handed. She writes him yet again, saying to Llewelyn, "He's probably got very busy?" and here I am fetching the mail every day before she gets home, one letter after another into the blue box. I don't even read them anymore. I don't even know why I'm doing it anymore.

The stone in my shoe.

Llewelyn catches me. Here's my chance to set myself right, to stop, to allow Sara to have him, to have love, life. Instead, I convince Llewleyn that this is the right thing to do, protect the child from pain. Love is pain. Don't you know? And dear, dim Llewelyn agrees with me because she only wants to please. Pleasing is love to Llewelyn. To have pleased is as far as her car goes. She conspires. The stone in my shoe.

There are many ways to die and by now I have known most. It is raining, sheeting down the windows in a grey wash. Sara is writing her final letter at the rolltop desk, her face damp, her shoulders shuttering under her dress. She has given up. Llewelyn watches me across the room and I see little lights in her brain coming on. Considering for the first time, perhaps, that I may be wrong, that I the eldest, the matron, mother to us all, have been wrong. Her eyes burn into me, a new intelligence flickering there, born of suffering, born of her sister's suffering.

I tell her, "The least you could do is make Sara a cup of tea," which she does. See how she reverts so quickly, how her new thinking – thinking for herself – drops to the floor like a napkin from her lap when she stands and goes into the kitchen to make her sister some tea.

Sara finishes her letter and runs down the stairs with it. She cannot move fast enough from her sorrow, her confusion, him, us out of The Nottingham, straight into the street and in front of the streetcar. By the sounds carrying up from the street we know just what has happened.

Within minutes I am standing on the curb. I watch for the ambulance though it is too late for an ambulance. Llewelyn arranges Sara's skirt on the street as though it were a bed and pats her hair. She picks the letter from where it landed near the gutter and hands it to me. I put it in the pocket of my blue sweater. There is a letter in the pocket of my sweater. There are more in the blue box upstairs. There is a stone in my shoe. There are so many ways to die. Sara luminous and beautiful on her back in the street. She will die but she will never dissolve in plain sight, like us. We are the sisters in Apt. 3B. You never see us. You will never see us.

Rebecca Rotert received her MA from Hollins College in Virginia Her work has appeared in Santa Clara Review, America Magazine, Hospital Drive Journal, Temenos Journal, Outside In Magazine *and* The New York Times. *The essay "Proteus on the Vasa" was nominated for a Pushcart Prize. Her novel,* Last Night at the Blue Angel, *was published by HarperCollins in 2014.*

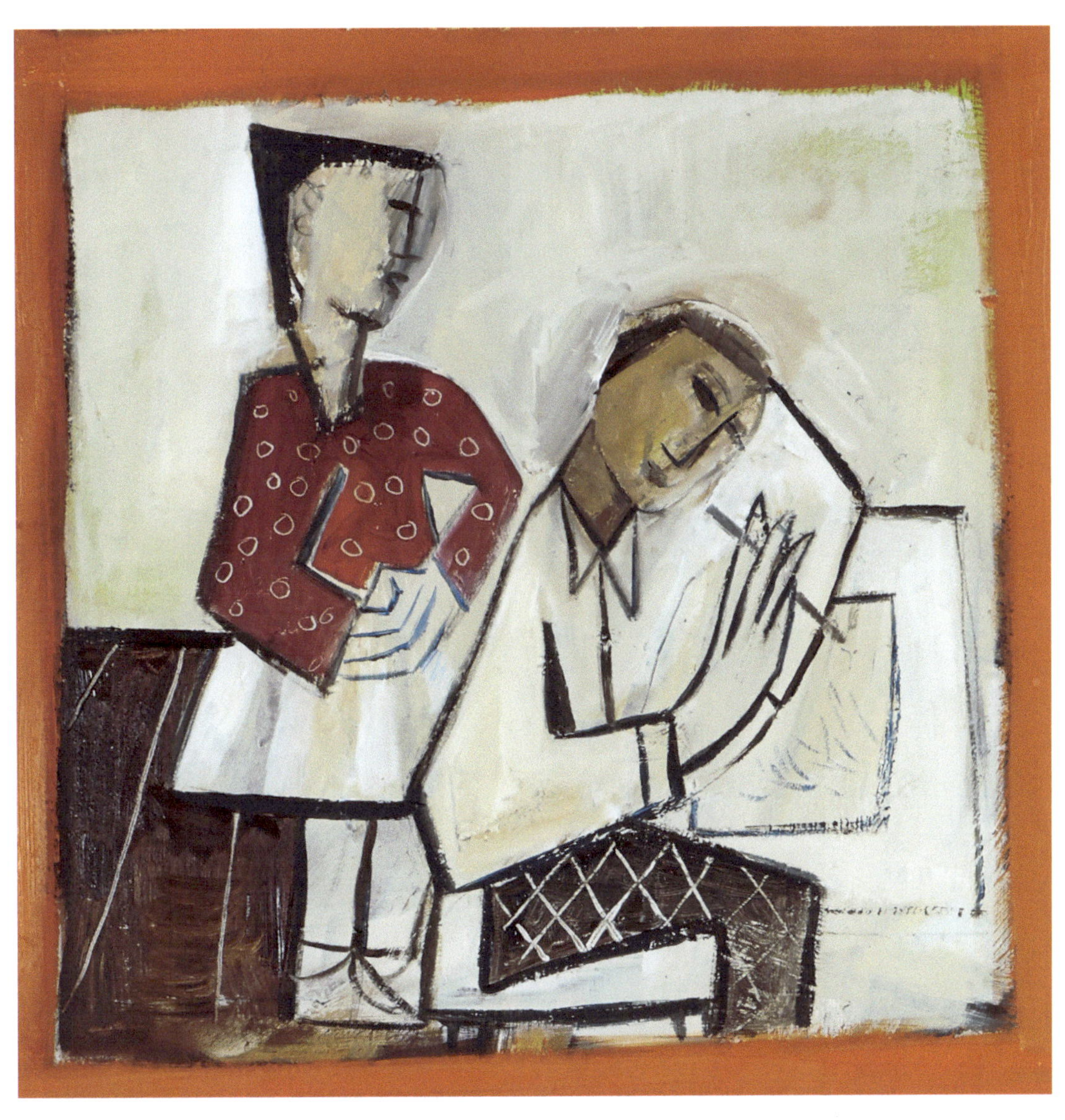

Sonnets of the Second Trimester | Devel Crisp

How blest we are to bear a daughter's grace!
The sound waves yield her healthy and alert.
Alas, to raise a child within this place,
These stark confines of 33rd and Burt.
Mere blocks away, the sirens pierce the night.
An endless reign of crownless kings and queens.
They're warriors, confused with how to fight.
Shots wake the alcoholics and the fiends.
We dare to bring a baby into this?
When chaos is our daily point-of-view.
I dread, but then, I'm lucky to admit,
It is a brighter space, because of you.
    No other place on earth I'd rather be.
    For in this place, a two became a three.

Our fights are few, but when we do, we scar.
Sometimes, the question wails, "Are we okay?"
No marriage, our foundation is vanguard.
Phenomenally, we decide to stay.
Financially, we're barely scraping by.
Pennies, so stretched, that we see Lincoln's pores.
Due rent and bills invade our troubled sky.
Don't know how long the landlord will endure.
Everyone will have their own opinions.
Our fam'lies, bless their hearts, they do mean well.
But we know what's best for our new infant.
Surviving on, we learn about ourselves.
    Through rough terrain, on grows our precious seed,
    Reminding us that faith is all we need.

Despite our lack, I know we'll be happy.
No matter what statistics try to prove.
We've found the way to keep our souls laughing,
If either shack or mansion we should move.
I wonder if she'll have your buoyant smile.
You ponder if her hair will curl like mine.
We hope, like us, she's cautious, strays from guile.
She won't, so she'll be perfect by design.

Her name shall be as beautiful as love.
No syllable off-rhythm we'll allow!
Feminine, but bold, rolls off of the tongue,
A pleasure to the world when spoke aloud.
        Who cares whatever evil is contrived?
        A few more months, our Heroine arrives!

Devel Crisp enjoys creating creative creations in Omaha, Nebraska, where he is an edutainer, father, and dreamer.

burnt books is the newest imprint of Spark Wheel Press (SWP) under the Nebraska Writers Collective. burnt books has a specific mission of celebrating local authors and artists, and *The History of a Day* is our first project.

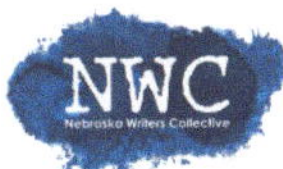

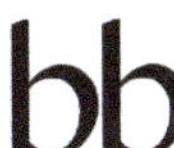

www.ingramcontent.com/pod-product-compliance
Lightning Source LLC
LaVergne TN
LVHW071633100826
845154LV00008BA/139
9780989783736